BLOOD PRESS

MW00957438

NAME. _____

Date	AM		PM		Notes
	Blood pressure	Pulse	Blood pressure	Pulse	

Level of Severity	Systolic	Diastolic
Normal	120	80
Mild Hypertension	140-160	90-100
Moderate Hypertension	160-200	100-120
Severe Hypertension	Above 200	160-200

BLOOD PRESSURE LOG

NAME. _____

Date	AM		PM		Notes
	Blood pressure	Pulse	Blood pressure	Pulse	

Level of Severity	Systolic	Diastolic
Normal	120	80
Mild Hypertension	140-160	90-100
Moderate Hypertension	160-200	100-120
Severe Hypertension	Above 200	160-200

BLOOD PRESSURE LOG

NAME. ....

Date	AM		PM		Notes
	Blood pressure	Pulse	Blood pressure	Pulse	

Level of Severity	Systolic	Diastolic
Normal	120	80
Mild Hypertension	140-160	90-100
Moderate Hypertension	160-200	100-120
Severe Hypertension	Above 200	160-200

BLOOD PRESSURE LOG

NAME. ....

Date	AM		PM		Notes
	Blood pressure	Pulse	Blood pressure	Pulse	

Level of Severity	Systolic	Diastolic
Normal	120	80
Mild Hypertension	140-160	90-100
Moderate Hypertension	160-200	100-120
Severe Hypertension	Above 200	160-200

BLOOD PRESSURE LOG

NAME. _____

Date	AM		PM		Notes
	Blood pressure	Pulse	Blood pressure	Pulse	

Level of Severity	Systolic	Diastolic
Normal	120	80
Mild Hypertension	140-160	90-100
Moderate Hypertension	160-200	100-120
Severe Hypertension	Above 200	160-200

BLOOD PRESSURE LOG

NAME. _____

Date	AM		PM		Notes
	Blood pressure	Pulse	Blood pressure	Pulse	

Level of Severity	Systolic	Diastolic
Normal	120	80
Mild Hypertension	140-160	90-100
Moderate Hypertension	160-200	100-120
Severe Hypertension	Above 200	160-200

BLOOD PRESSURE LOG

NAME.

Date	AM		PM		Notes
	Blood pressure	Pulse	Blood pressure	Pulse	

Level of Severity	Systolic	Diastolic
Normal	120	80
Mild Hypertension	140-160	90-100
Moderate Hypertension	160-200	100-120
Severe Hypertension	Above 200	160-200

BLOOD PRESSURE LOG

NAME. ....

Date	AM		PM		Notes
	Blood pressure	Pulse	Blood pressure	Pulse	

Level of Severity	Systolic	Diastolic
Normal	120	80
Mild Hypertension	140-160	90-100
Moderate Hypertension	160-200	100-120
Severe Hypertension	Above 200	160-200

BLOOD PRESSURE LOG

NAME.

Date	AM		PM		Notes
	Blood pressure	Pulse	Blood pressure	Pulse	

Level of Severity	Systolic	Diastolic
Normal	120	80
Mild Hypertension	140-160	90-100
Moderate Hypertension	160-200	100-120
Severe Hypertension	Above 200	160-200

BLOOD PRESSURE LOG

NAME. _____

Date	AM		PM		Notes
	Blood pressure	Pulse	Blood pressure	Pulse	

Level of Severity	Systolic	Diastolic
Normal	120	80
Mild Hypertension	140-160	90-100
Moderate Hypertension	160-200	100-120
Severe Hypertension	Above 200	160-200

BLOOD PRESSURE LOG

NAME. _____

Date	AM		PM		Notes
	Blood pressure	Pulse	Blood pressure	Pulse	

Level of Severity	Systolic	Diastolic
Normal	120	80
Mild Hypertension	140-160	90-100
Moderate Hypertension	160-200	100-120
Severe Hypertension	Above 200	160-200

BLOOD PRESSURE LOG

NAME. _____

Date	AM		PM		Notes
	Blood pressure	Pulse	Blood pressure	Pulse	

Level of Severity	Systolic	Diastolic
Normal	120	80
Mild Hypertension	140-160	90-100
Moderate Hypertension	160-200	100-120
Severe Hypertension	Above 200	160-200

BLOOD PRESSURE LOG

NAME. _____

Date	AM		PM		Notes
	Blood pressure	Pulse	Blood pressure	Pulse	

Level of Severity	Systolic	Diastolic
Normal	120	80
Mild Hypertension	140-160	90-100
Moderate Hypertension	160-200	100-120
Severe Hypertension	Above 200	160-200

BLOOD PRESSURE LOG

NAME. ....

Date	AM		PM		Notes
	Blood pressure	Pulse	Blood pressure	Pulse	

Level of Severity	Systolic	Diastolic
Normal	120	80
Mild Hypertension	140-160	90-100
Moderate Hypertension	160-200	100-120
Severe Hypertension	Above 200	160-200

BLOOD PRESSURE LOG

NAME. _____

Date	AM		PM		Notes
	Blood pressure	Pulse	Blood pressure	Pulse	

Level of Severity	Systolic	Diastolic
Normal	120	80
Mild Hypertension	140-160	90-100
Moderate Hypertension	160-200	100-120
Severe Hypertension	Above 200	160-200

BLOOD PRESSURE LOG

NAME. _____

Date	AM		PM		Notes
	Blood pressure	Pulse	Blood pressure	Pulse	

Level of Severity	Systolic	Diastolic
Normal	120	80
Mild Hypertension	140-160	90-100
Moderate Hypertension	160-200	100-120
Severe Hypertension	Above 200	160-200

BLOOD PRESSURE LOG

NAME. _____

Date	AM		PM		Notes
	Blood pressure	Pulse	Blood pressure	Pulse	

Level of Severity	Systolic	Diastolic
Normal	120	80
Mild Hypertension	140-160	90-100
Moderate Hypertension	160-200	100-120
Severe Hypertension	Above 200	160-200

BLOOD PRESSURE LOG

NAME. _____

Date	AM		PM		Notes
	Blood pressure	Pulse	Blood pressure	Pulse	

Level of Severity	Systolic	Diastolic
Normal	120	80
Mild Hypertension	140-160	90-100
Moderate Hypertension	160-200	100-120
Severe Hypertension	Above 200	160-200

BLOOD PRESSURE LOG

NAME. _____

Date	AM		PM		Notes
	Blood pressure	Pulse	Blood pressure	Pulse	

Level of Severity	Systolic	Diastolic
Normal	120	80
Mild Hypertension	140-160	90-100
Moderate Hypertension	160-200	100-120
Severe Hypertension	Above 200	160-200

BLOOD PRESSURE LOG

NAME. ....

Date	AM		PM		Notes
	Blood pressure	Pulse	Blood pressure	Pulse	

Level of Severity	Systolic	Diastolic
Normal	120	80
Mild Hypertension	140-160	90-100
Moderate Hypertension	160-200	100-120
Severe Hypertension	Above 200	160-200

BLOOD PRESSURE LOG

NAME. _____

Date	AM		PM		Notes
	Blood pressure	Pulse	Blood pressure	Pulse	

Level of Severity	Systolic	Diastolic
Normal	120	80
Mild Hypertension	140-160	90-100
Moderate Hypertension	160-200	100-120
Severe Hypertension	Above 200	160-200

BLOOD PRESSURE LOG

NAME. ....

Date	AM		PM		Notes
	Blood pressure	Pulse	Blood pressure	Pulse	

Level of Severity	Systolic	Diastolic
Normal	120	80
Mild Hypertension	140-160	90-100
Moderate Hypertension	160-200	100-120
Severe Hypertension	Above 200	160-200

BLOOD PRESSURE LOG

NAME. ....

Date	AM		PM		Notes
	Blood pressure	Pulse	Blood pressure	Pulse	

Level of Severity	Systolic	Diastolic
Normal	120	80
Mild Hypertension	140-160	90-100
Moderate Hypertension	160-200	100-120
Severe Hypertension	Above 200	160-200

BLOOD PRESSURE LOG

NAME. ....

Date	AM		PM		Notes
	Blood pressure	Pulse	Blood pressure	Pulse	

Level of Severity	Systolic	Diastolic
Normal	120	80
Mild Hypertension	140-160	90-100
Moderate Hypertension	160-200	100-120
Severe Hypertension	Above 200	160-200

BLOOD PRESSURE LOG

NAME.

Date	AM		PM		Notes
	Blood pressure	Pulse	Blood pressure	Pulse	

Level of Severity	Systolic	Diastolic
Normal	120	80
Mild Hypertension	140-160	90-100
Moderate Hypertension	160-200	100-120
Severe Hypertension	Above 200	160-200

BLOOD PRESSURE LOG

NAME. _____

Date	AM		PM		Notes
	Blood pressure	Pulse	Blood pressure	Pulse	

Level of Severity	Systolic	Diastolic
Normal	120	80
Mild Hypertension	140-160	90-100
Moderate Hypertension	160-200	100-120
Severe Hypertension	Above 200	160-200

BLOOD PRESSURE LOG

NAME. _____

Date	AM		PM		Notes
	Blood pressure	Pulse	Blood pressure	Pulse	

Level of Severity	Systolic	Diastolic
Normal	120	80
Mild Hypertension	140-160	90-100
Moderate Hypertension	160-200	100-120
Severe Hypertension	Above 200	160-200

BLOOD PRESSURE LOG

NAME.

Date	AM		PM		Notes
	Blood pressure	Pulse	Blood pressure	Pulse	

Level of Severity	Systolic	Diastolic
Normal	120	80
Mild Hypertension	140-160	90-100
Moderate Hypertension	160-200	100-120
Severe Hypertension	Above 200	160-200

BLOOD PRESSURE LOG

NAME.

Date	AM		PM		Notes
	Blood pressure	Pulse	Blood pressure	Pulse	

Level of Severity	Systolic	Diastolic
Normal	120	80
Mild Hypertension	140-160	90-100
Moderate Hypertension	160-200	100-120
Severe Hypertension	Above 200	160-200

BLOOD PRESSURE LOG

NAME.

Date	AM		PM		Notes
	Blood pressure	Pulse	Blood pressure	Pulse	

Level of Severity	Systolic	Diastolic
Normal	120	80
Mild Hypertension	140-160	90-100
Moderate Hypertension	160-200	100-120
Severe Hypertension	Above 200	160-200

BLOOD PRESSURE LOG

NAME. ....

Date	AM		PM		Notes
	Blood pressure	Pulse	Blood pressure	Pulse	

Level of Severity	Systolic	Diastolic
Normal	120	80
Mild Hypertension	140-160	90-100
Moderate Hypertension	160-200	100-120
Severe Hypertension	Above 200	160-200

BLOOD PRESSURE LOG

NAME. ....

Date	AM		PM		Notes
	Blood pressure	Pulse	Blood pressure	Pulse	

Level of Severity	Systolic	Diastolic
Normal	120	80
Mild Hypertension	140-160	90-100
Moderate Hypertension	160-200	100-120
Severe Hypertension	Above 200	160-200

BLOOD PRESSURE LOG

NAME.

Date	AM		PM		Notes
	Blood pressure	Pulse	Blood pressure	Pulse	

Level of Severity	Systolic	Diastolic
Normal	120	80
Mild Hypertension	140-160	90-100
Moderate Hypertension	160-200	100-120
Severe Hypertension	Above 200	160-200

BLOOD PRESSURE LOG

NAME. ....

Date	AM		PM		Notes
	Blood pressure	Pulse	Blood pressure	Pulse	

Level of Severity	Systolic	Diastolic
Normal	120	80
Mild Hypertension	140-160	90-100
Moderate Hypertension	160-200	100-120
Severe Hypertension	Above 200	160-200

BLOOD PRESSURE LOG

NAME. _____

Date	AM		PM		Notes
	Blood pressure	Pulse	Blood pressure	Pulse	

Level of Severity	Systolic	Diastolic
Normal	120	80
Mild Hypertension	140-160	90-100
Moderate Hypertension	160-200	100-120
Severe Hypertension	Above 200	160-200

BLOOD PRESSURE LOG

NAME. ....

Date	AM		PM		Notes
	Blood pressure	Pulse	Blood pressure	Pulse	

Level of Severity	Systolic	Diastolic
Normal	120	80
Mild Hypertension	140-160	90-100
Moderate Hypertension	160-200	100-120
Severe Hypertension	Above 200	160-200

- -
- -
- -
- -

- -
- -
- -
- -
- -

BLOOD PRESSURE LOG

NAME.

Date	AM		PM		Notes
	Blood pressure	Pulse	Blood pressure	Pulse	

Level of Severity	Systolic	Diastolic
Normal	120	80
Mild Hypertension	140-160	90-100
Moderate Hypertension	160-200	100-120
Severe Hypertension	Above 200	160-200

BLOOD PRESSURE LOG

NAME. _____

Date	AM		PM		Notes
	Blood pressure	Pulse	Blood pressure	Pulse	

Level of Severity	Systolic	Diastolic
Normal	120	80
Mild Hypertension	140-160	90-100
Moderate Hypertension	160-200	100-120
Severe Hypertension	Above 200	160-200

_____
_____
_____
_____
_____
_____
_____
_____

BLOOD PRESSURE LOG

NAME. _____

Date	AM		PM		Notes
	Blood pressure	Pulse	Blood pressure	Pulse	

Level of Severity	Systolic	Diastolic
Normal	120	80
Mild Hypertension	140-160	90-100
Moderate Hypertension	160-200	100-120
Severe Hypertension	Above 200	160-200

BLOOD PRESSURE LOG

NAME. _____

Date	AM		PM		Notes
	Blood pressure	Pulse	Blood pressure	Pulse	

Level of Severity	Systolic	Diastolic
Normal	120	80
Mild Hypertension	140-160	90-100
Moderate Hypertension	160-200	100-120
Severe Hypertension	Above 200	160-200

BLOOD PRESSURE LOG

NAME. ....

Date	AM		PM		Notes
	Blood pressure	Pulse	Blood pressure	Pulse	

Level of Severity	Systolic	Diastolic
Normal	120	80
Mild Hypertension	140-160	90-100
Moderate Hypertension	160-200	100-120
Severe Hypertension	Above 200	160-200

BLOOD PRESSURE LOG

NAME. _____

Date	AM		PM		Notes
	Blood pressure	Pulse	Blood pressure	Pulse	

Level of Severity	Systolic	Diastolic
Normal	120	80
Mild Hypertension	140-160	90-100
Moderate Hypertension	160-200	100-120
Severe Hypertension	Above 200	160-200

BLOOD PRESSURE LOG

NAME. _____

Date	AM		PM		Notes
	Blood pressure	Pulse	Blood pressure	Pulse	

Level of Severity	Systolic	Diastolic
Normal	120	80
Mild Hypertension	140-160	90-100
Moderate Hypertension	160-200	100-120
Severe Hypertension	Above 200	160-200

BLOOD PRESSURE LOG

NAME. ....

Date	AM		PM		Notes
	Blood pressure	Pulse	Blood pressure	Pulse	

Level of Severity	Systolic	Diastolic
Normal	120	80
Mild Hypertension	140-160	90-100
Moderate Hypertension	160-200	100-120
Severe Hypertension	Above 200	160-200

BLOOD PRESSURE LOG

NAME. _____

Date	AM		PM		Notes
	Blood pressure	Pulse	Blood pressure	Pulse	

Level of Severity	Systolic	Diastolic
Normal	120	80
Mild Hypertension	140-160	90-100
Moderate Hypertension	160-200	100-120
Severe Hypertension	Above 200	160-200

BLOOD PRESSURE LOG

NAME. _____

Date	AM		PM		Notes
	Blood pressure	Pulse	Blood pressure	Pulse	

Level of Severity	Systolic	Diastolic
Normal	120	80
Mild Hypertension	140-160	90-100
Moderate Hypertension	160-200	100-120
Severe Hypertension	Above 200	160-200

BLOOD PRESSURE LOG

NAME. _____

Date	AM		PM		Notes
	Blood pressure	Pulse	Blood pressure	Pulse	

Level of Severity	Systolic	Diastolic
Normal	120	80
Mild Hypertension	140-160	90-100
Moderate Hypertension	160-200	100-120
Severe Hypertension	Above 200	160-200

BLOOD PRESSURE LOG

NAME. _____

Date	AM		PM		Notes
	Blood pressure	Pulse	Blood pressure	Pulse	

Level of Severity	Systolic	Diastolic
Normal	120	80
Mild Hypertension	140-160	90-100
Moderate Hypertension	160-200	100-120
Severe Hypertension	Above 200	160-200

Blood Pressure Log

NAME. _____

Date	AM		PM		Notes
	Blood pressure	Pulse	Blood pressure	Pulse	

Level of Severity	Systolic	Diastolic
Normal	120	80
Mild Hypertension	140-160	90-100
Moderate Hypertension	160-200	100-120
Severe Hypertension	Above 200	160-200

BLOOD PRESSURE LOG

NAME. _____

Date	AM		PM		Notes
	Blood pressure	Pulse	Blood pressure	Pulse	

Level of Severity	Systolic	Diastolic
Normal	120	80
Mild Hypertension	140-160	90-100
Moderate Hypertension	160-200	100-120
Severe Hypertension	Above 200	160-200

BLOOD PRESSURE LOG

NAME. ....

Date	AM		PM		Notes
	Blood pressure	Pulse	Blood pressure	Pulse	

Level of Severity	Systolic	Diastolic
Normal	120	80
Mild Hypertension	140-160	90-100
Moderate Hypertension	160-200	100-120
Severe Hypertension	Above 200	160-200

BLOOD PRESSURE LOG

NAME. _____

Date	AM		PM		Notes
	Blood pressure	Pulse	Blood pressure	Pulse	

Level of Severity	Systolic	Diastolic
Normal	120	80
Mild Hypertension	140-160	90-100
Moderate Hypertension	160-200	100-120
Severe Hypertension	Above 200	160-200

Blood Pressure Log

NAME. _____

Date	AM		PM		Notes
	Blood pressure	Pulse	Blood pressure	Pulse	

Level of Severity	Systolic	Diastolic
Normal	120	80
Mild Hypertension	140-160	90-100
Moderate Hypertension	160-200	100-120
Severe Hypertension	Above 200	160-200

BLOOD PRESSURE LOG

NAME.

Date	AM		PM		Notes
	Blood pressure	Pulse	Blood pressure	Pulse	

Level of Severity	Systolic	Diastolic
Normal	120	80
Mild Hypertension	140-160	90-100
Moderate Hypertension	160-200	100-120
Severe Hypertension	Above 200	160-200

BLOOD PRESSURE LOG

NAME. ....

Date	AM		PM		Notes
	Blood pressure	Pulse	Blood pressure	Pulse	

Level of Severity	Systolic	Diastolic
Normal	120	80
Mild Hypertension	140-160	90-100
Moderate Hypertension	160-200	100-120
Severe Hypertension	Above 200	160-200

BLOOD PRESSURE LOG

NAME. _____

Date	AM		PM		Notes
	Blood pressure	Pulse	Blood pressure	Pulse	

Level of Severity	Systolic	Diastolic
Normal	120	80
Mild Hypertension	140-160	90-100
Moderate Hypertension	160-200	100-120
Severe Hypertension	Above 200	160-200

BLOOD PRESSURE LOG

NAME.

Date	AM		PM		Notes
	Blood pressure	Pulse	Blood pressure	Pulse	

Level of Severity	Systolic	Diastolic
Normal	120	80
Mild Hypertension	140-160	90-100
Moderate Hypertension	160-200	100-120
Severe Hypertension	Above 200	160-200

BLOOD PRESSURE LOG

NAME. _____

Date	AM		PM		Notes
	Blood pressure	Pulse	Blood pressure	Pulse	

Level of Severity	Systolic	Diastolic
Normal	120	80
Mild Hypertension	140-160	90-100
Moderate Hypertension	160-200	100-120
Severe Hypertension	Above 200	160-200

BLOOD PRESSURE LOG

NAME. ....

Date	AM		PM		Notes
	Blood pressure	Pulse	Blood pressure	Pulse	

Level of Severity	Systolic	Diastolic
Normal	120	80
Mild Hypertension	140-160	90-100
Moderate Hypertension	160-200	100-120
Severe Hypertension	Above 200	160-200

BLOOD PRESSURE LOG

NAME. _____

Date	AM		PM		Notes
	Blood pressure	Pulse	Blood pressure	Pulse	

Level of Severity	Systolic	Diastolic
Normal	120	80
Mild Hypertension	140-160	90-100
Moderate Hypertension	160-200	100-120
Severe Hypertension	Above 200	160-200

BLOOD PRESSURE LOG

NAME. _____

Date	AM		PM		Notes
	Blood pressure	Pulse	Blood pressure	Pulse	

Level of Severity	Systolic	Diastolic
Normal	120	80
Mild Hypertension	140-160	90-100
Moderate Hypertension	160-200	100-120
Severe Hypertension	Above 200	160-200

BLOOD PRESSURE LOG

NAME. ....

Date	AM		PM		Notes
	Blood pressure	Pulse	Blood pressure	Pulse	

Level of Severity	Systolic	Diastolic
Normal	120	80
Mild Hypertension	140-160	90-100
Moderate Hypertension	160-200	100-120
Severe Hypertension	Above 200	160-200

BLOOD PRESSURE LOG

NAME. _____

Date	AM		PM		Notes
	Blood pressure	Pulse	Blood pressure	Pulse	

Level of Severity	Systolic	Diastolic
Normal	120	80
Mild Hypertension	140-160	90-100
Moderate Hypertension	160-200	100-120
Severe Hypertension	Above 200	160-200

BLOOD PRESSURE LOG

NAME. _____

Date	AM		PM		Notes
	Blood pressure	Pulse	Blood pressure	Pulse	

Level of Severity	Systolic	Diastolic
Normal	120	80
Mild Hypertension	140-160	90-100
Moderate Hypertension	160-200	100-120
Severe Hypertension	Above 200	160-200

BLOOD PRESSURE LOG

NAME. _____

Date	AM		PM		Notes
	Blood pressure	Pulse	Blood pressure	Pulse	

Level of Severity	Systolic	Diastolic
Normal	120	80
Mild Hypertension	140-160	90-100
Moderate Hypertension	160-200	100-120
Severe Hypertension	Above 200	160-200

BLOOD PRESSURE LOG

NAME. _____

Date	AM Blood pressure	AM Pulse	PM Blood pressure	PM Pulse	Notes

Level of Severity	Systolic	Diastolic
Normal	120	80
Mild Hypertension	140-160	90-100
Moderate Hypertension	160-200	100-120
Severe Hypertension	Above 200	160-200

BLOOD PRESSURE LOG

NAME.

Date	AM		PM		Notes
	Blood pressure	Pulse	Blood pressure	Pulse	

Level of Severity	Systolic	Diastolic
Normal	120	80
Mild Hypertension	140-160	90-100
Moderate Hypertension	160-200	100-120
Severe Hypertension	Above 200	160-200

BLOOD PRESSURE LOG

NAME. _____

Date	AM		PM		Notes
	Blood pressure	Pulse	Blood pressure	Pulse	

Level of Severity	Systolic	Diastolic
Normal	120	80
Mild Hypertension	140-160	90-100
Moderate Hypertension	160-200	100-120
Severe Hypertension	Above 200	160-200

Blood Pressure Log

NAME. _____

Date	AM		PM		Notes
	Blood pressure	Pulse	Blood pressure	Pulse	

Level of Severity	Systolic	Diastolic
Normal	120	80
Mild Hypertension	140-160	90-100
Moderate Hypertension	160-200	100-120
Severe Hypertension	Above 200	160-200

BLOOD PRESSURE LOG

NAME. _____

Date	AM		PM		Notes
	Blood pressure	Pulse	Blood pressure	Pulse	

Level of Severity	Systolic	Diastolic
Normal	120	80
Mild Hypertension	140-160	90-100
Moderate Hypertension	160-200	100-120
Severe Hypertension	Above 200	160-200

Blood Pressure Log

Name. ....

Date	AM		PM		Notes
	Blood pressure	Pulse	Blood pressure	Pulse	

Level of Severity	Systolic	Diastolic
Normal	120	80
Mild Hypertension	140-160	90-100
Moderate Hypertension	160-200	100-120
Severe Hypertension	Above 200	160-200

BLOOD PRESSURE LOG

NAME. _____

Date	AM		PM		Notes
	Blood pressure	Pulse	Blood pressure	Pulse	

Level of Severity	Systolic	Diastolic
Normal	120	80
Mild Hypertension	140-160	90-100
Moderate Hypertension	160-200	100-120
Severe Hypertension	Above 200	160-200

BLOOD PRESSURE LOG

NAME. ....

Date	AM		PM		Notes
	Blood pressure	Pulse	Blood pressure	Pulse	

Level of Severity	Systolic	Diastolic
Normal	120	80
Mild Hypertension	140-160	90-100
Moderate Hypertension	160-200	100-120
Severe Hypertension	Above 200	160-200

BLOOD PRESSURE LOG

NAME. _____

Date	AM		PM		Notes
	Blood pressure	Pulse	Blood pressure	Pulse	

Level of Severity	Systolic	Diastolic
Normal	120	80
Mild Hypertension	140-160	90-100
Moderate Hypertension	160-200	100-120
Severe Hypertension	Above 200	160-200

BLOOD PRESSURE LOG

NAME. _____

Date	AM		PM		Notes
	Blood pressure	Pulse	Blood pressure	Pulse	

Level of Severity	Systolic	Diastolic
Normal	120	80
Mild Hypertension	140-160	90-100
Moderate Hypertension	160-200	100-120
Severe Hypertension	Above 200	160-200

BLOOD PRESSURE LOG

NAME. _____

Date	AM		PM		Notes
	Blood pressure	Pulse	Blood pressure	Pulse	

Level of Severity	Systolic	Diastolic
Normal	120	80
Mild Hypertension	140-160	90-100
Moderate Hypertension	160-200	100-120
Severe Hypertension	Above 200	160-200

Blood Pressure Log

Name. ....

Date	AM		PM		Notes
	Blood pressure	Pulse	Blood pressure	Pulse	

Level of Severity	Systolic	Diastolic
Normal	120	80
Mild Hypertension	140-160	90-100
Moderate Hypertension	160-200	100-120
Severe Hypertension	Above 200	160-200

BLOOD PRESSURE LOG

NAME. _____

Date	AM		PM		Notes
	Blood pressure	Pulse	Blood pressure	Pulse	

Level of Severity	Systolic	Diastolic
Normal	120	80
Mild Hypertension	140-160	90-100
Moderate Hypertension	160-200	100-120
Severe Hypertension	Above 200	160-200

BLOOD PRESSURE LOG

NAME. _____

Date	AM		PM		Notes
	Blood pressure	Pulse	Blood pressure	Pulse	

Level of Severity	Systolic	Diastolic
Normal	120	80
Mild Hypertension	140-160	90-100
Moderate Hypertension	160-200	100-120
Severe Hypertension	Above 200	160-200

BLOOD PRESSURE LOG

NAME. _____

Date	AM		PM		Notes
	Blood pressure	Pulse	Blood pressure	Pulse	

Level of Severity	Systolic	Diastolic
Normal	120	80
Mild Hypertension	140-160	90-100
Moderate Hypertension	160-200	100-120
Severe Hypertension	Above 200	160-200

BLOOD PRESSURE LOG

NAME. _____

Date	AM		PM		Notes
	Blood pressure	Pulse	Blood pressure	Pulse	

Level of Severity	Systolic	Diastolic
Normal	120	80
Mild Hypertension	140-160	90-100
Moderate Hypertension	160-200	100-120
Severe Hypertension	Above 200	160-200

BLOOD PRESSURE LOG

NAME. _____

Date	AM		PM		Notes
	Blood pressure	Pulse	Blood pressure	Pulse	

Level of Severity	Systolic	Diastolic
Normal	120	80
Mild Hypertension	140-160	90-100
Moderate Hypertension	160-200	100-120
Severe Hypertension	Above 200	160-200

BLOOD PRESSURE LOG

NAME. ....

Date	AM		PM		Notes
	Blood pressure	Pulse	Blood pressure	Pulse	

Level of Severity	Systolic	Diastolic
Normal	120	80
Mild Hypertension	140-160	90-100
Moderate Hypertension	160-200	100-120
Severe Hypertension	Above 200	160-200

BLOOD PRESSURE LOG

NAME.

Date	AM		PM		Notes
	Blood pressure	Pulse	Blood pressure	Pulse	

Level of Severity	Systolic	Diastolic
Normal	120	80
Mild Hypertension	140-160	90-100
Moderate Hypertension	160-200	100-120
Severe Hypertension	Above 200	160-200

BLOOD PRESSURE LOG

NAME. _____

Date	AM		PM		Notes
	Blood pressure	Pulse	Blood pressure	Pulse	

Level of Severity	Systolic	Diastolic
Normal	120	80
Mild Hypertension	140-160	90-100
Moderate Hypertension	160-200	100-120
Severe Hypertension	Above 200	160-200

BLOOD PRESSURE LOG

NAME. _____

Date	AM		PM		Notes
	Blood pressure	Pulse	Blood pressure	Pulse	

Level of Severity	Systolic	Diastolic
Normal	120	80
Mild Hypertension	140-160	90-100
Moderate Hypertension	160-200	100-120
Severe Hypertension	Above 200	160-200

BLOOD PRESSURE LOG

NAME. _____

Date	AM		PM		Notes
	Blood pressure	Pulse	Blood pressure	Pulse	

Level of Severity	Systolic	Diastolic
Normal	120	80
Mild Hypertension	140-160	90-100
Moderate Hypertension	160-200	100-120
Severe Hypertension	Above 200	160-200

BLOOD PRESSURE LOG

NAME. _____

Date	AM		PM		Notes
	Blood pressure	Pulse	Blood pressure	Pulse	

Level of Severity	Systolic	Diastolic
Normal	120	80
Mild Hypertension	140-160	90-100
Moderate Hypertension	160-200	100-120
Severe Hypertension	Above 200	160-200

BLOOD PRESSURE LOG

NAME. _____

Date	AM		PM		Notes
	Blood pressure	Pulse	Blood pressure	Pulse	

Level of Severity	Systolic	Diastolic
Normal	120	80
Mild Hypertension	140-160	90-100
Moderate Hypertension	160-200	100-120
Severe Hypertension	Above 200	160-200

BLOOD PRESSURE LOG

NAME. _____

Date	AM		PM		Notes
	Blood pressure	Pulse	Blood pressure	Pulse	

Level of Severity	Systolic	Diastolic
Normal	120	80
Mild Hypertension	140-160	90-100
Moderate Hypertension	160-200	100-120
Severe Hypertension	Above 200	160-200

BLOOD PRESSURE LOG

NAME. _____

Date	AM		PM		Notes
	Blood pressure	Pulse	Blood pressure	Pulse	

Level of Severity	Systolic	Diastolic
Normal	120	80
Mild Hypertension	140-160	90-100
Moderate Hypertension	160-200	100-120
Severe Hypertension	Above 200	160-200

BLOOD PRESSURE LOG

NAME.

Date	AM		PM		Notes
	Blood pressure	Pulse	Blood pressure	Pulse	

Level of Severity	Systolic	Diastolic
Normal	120	80
Mild Hypertension	140-160	90-100
Moderate Hypertension	160-200	100-120
Severe Hypertension	Above 200	160-200

Blood Pressure Log

Name. _____

Date	AM		PM		Notes
	Blood pressure	Pulse	Blood pressure	Pulse	

Level of Severity	Systolic	Diastolic
Normal	120	80
Mild Hypertension	140-160	90-100
Moderate Hypertension	160-200	100-120
Severe Hypertension	Above 200	160-200

BLOOD PRESSURE LOG

NAME. _____

Date	AM		PM		Notes
	Blood pressure	Pulse	Blood pressure	Pulse	

Level of Severity	Systolic	Diastolic
Normal	120	80
Mild Hypertension	140-160	90-100
Moderate Hypertension	160-200	100-120
Severe Hypertension	Above 200	160-200

BLOOD PRESSURE LOG

NAME. ....

Date	AM		PM		Notes
	Blood pressure	Pulse	Blood pressure	Pulse	

Level of Severity	Systolic	Diastolic
Normal	120	80
Mild Hypertension	140-160	90-100
Moderate Hypertension	160-200	100-120
Severe Hypertension	Above 200	160-200

BLOOD PRESSURE LOG

NAME. _____

Date	AM		PM		Notes
	Blood pressure	Pulse	Blood pressure	Pulse	

Level of Severity	Systolic	Diastolic
Normal	120	80
Mild Hypertension	140-160	90-100
Moderate Hypertension	160-200	100-120
Severe Hypertension	Above 200	160-200

BLOOD PRESSURE LOG

NAME. _____

Date	AM		PM		Notes
	Blood pressure	Pulse	Blood pressure	Pulse	

Level of Severity	Systolic	Diastolic
Normal	120	80
Mild Hypertension	140-160	90-100
Moderate Hypertension	160-200	100-120
Severe Hypertension	Above 200	160-200

BLOOD PRESSURE LOG

NAME. _____

Date	AM		PM		Notes
	Blood pressure	Pulse	Blood pressure	Pulse	

Level of Severity	Systolic	Diastolic
Normal	120	80
Mild Hypertension	140-160	90-100
Moderate Hypertension	160-200	100-120
Severe Hypertension	Above 200	160-200

BLOOD PRESSURE LOG

NAME.

Date	AM		PM		Notes
	Blood pressure	Pulse	Blood pressure	Pulse	

Level of Severity	Systolic	Diastolic
Normal	120	80
Mild Hypertension	140-160	90-100
Moderate Hypertension	160-200	100-120
Severe Hypertension	Above 200	160-200

BLOOD PRESSURE LOG

NAME. _____

Date	AM		PM		Notes
	Blood pressure	Pulse	Blood pressure	Pulse	

Level of Severity	Systolic	Diastolic
Normal	120	80
Mild Hypertension	140-160	90-100
Moderate Hypertension	160-200	100-120
Severe Hypertension	Above 200	160-200

BLOOD PRESSURE LOG

NAME. _____

Date	AM		PM		Notes
	Blood pressure	Pulse	Blood pressure	Pulse	

Level of Severity	Systolic	Diastolic
Normal	120	80
Mild Hypertension	140-160	90-100
Moderate Hypertension	160-200	100-120
Severe Hypertension	Above 200	160-200

BLOOD PRESSURE LOG

NAME. _____

Date	AM		PM		Notes
	Blood pressure	Pulse	Blood pressure	Pulse	

Level of Severity	Systolic	Diastolic
Normal	120	80
Mild Hypertension	140-160	90-100
Moderate Hypertension	160-200	100-120
Severe Hypertension	Above 200	160-200

BLOOD PRESSURE LOG

NAME. ....

Date	AM		PM		Notes
	Blood pressure	Pulse	Blood pressure	Pulse	

Level of Severity	Systolic	Diastolic
Normal	120	80
Mild Hypertension	140-160	90-100
Moderate Hypertension	160-200	100-120
Severe Hypertension	Above 200	160-200

BLOOD PRESSURE LOG

NAME. _____

Date	AM		PM		Notes
	Blood pressure	Pulse	Blood pressure	Pulse	

Level of Severity	Systolic	Diastolic
Normal	120	80
Mild Hypertension	140-160	90-100
Moderate Hypertension	160-200	100-120
Severe Hypertension	Above 200	160-200

BLOOD PRESSURE LOG

NAME. _____

Date	AM		PM		Notes
	Blood pressure	Pulse	Blood pressure	Pulse	

Level of Severity	Systolic	Diastolic
Normal	120	80
Mild Hypertension	140-160	90-100
Moderate Hypertension	160-200	100-120
Severe Hypertension	Above 200	160-200

BLOOD PRESSURE LOG

NAME. _____

Date	AM		PM		Notes
	Blood pressure	Pulse	Blood pressure	Pulse	

Level of Severity	Systolic	Diastolic
Normal	120	80
Mild Hypertension	140-160	90-100
Moderate Hypertension	160-200	100-120
Severe Hypertension	Above 200	160-200

Blood Pressure Log

NAME. _____

Date	AM		PM		Notes
	Blood pressure	Pulse	Blood pressure	Pulse	

Level of Severity	Systolic	Diastolic
Normal	120	80
Mild Hypertension	140-160	90-100
Moderate Hypertension	160-200	100-120
Severe Hypertension	Above 200	160-200

BLOOD PRESSURE LOG

NAME. _____

Date	AM		PM		Notes
	Blood pressure	Pulse	Blood pressure	Pulse	

Level of Severity	Systolic	Diastolic
Normal	120	80
Mild Hypertension	140-160	90-100
Moderate Hypertension	160-200	100-120
Severe Hypertension	Above 200	160-200

BLOOD PRESSURE LOG

NAME. _____

Date	AM		PM		Notes
	Blood pressure	Pulse	Blood pressure	Pulse	

Level of Severity	Systolic	Diastolic
Normal	120	80
Mild Hypertension	140-160	90-100
Moderate Hypertension	160-200	100-120
Severe Hypertension	Above 200	160-200

BLOOD PRESSURE LOG

NAME. _____

Date	AM		PM		Notes
	Blood pressure	Pulse	Blood pressure	Pulse	

Level of Severity	Systolic	Diastolic
Normal	120	80
Mild Hypertension	140-160	90-100
Moderate Hypertension	160-200	100-120
Severe Hypertension	Above 200	160-200

BLOOD PRESSURE LOG

NAME. _____

Date	AM		PM		Notes
	Blood pressure	Pulse	Blood pressure	Pulse	

Level of Severity	Systolic	Diastolic
Normal	120	80
Mild Hypertension	140-160	90-100
Moderate Hypertension	160-200	100-120
Severe Hypertension	Above 200	160-200

BLOOD PRESSURE LOG

NAME. _____

Date	AM		PM		Notes
	Blood pressure	Pulse	Blood pressure	Pulse	

Level of Severity	Systolic	Diastolic
Normal	120	80
Mild Hypertension	140-160	90-100
Moderate Hypertension	160-200	100-120
Severe Hypertension	Above 200	160-200

BLOOD PRESSURE LOG

NAME. _____

Date	AM		PM		Notes
	Blood pressure	Pulse	Blood pressure	Pulse	

Level of Severity	Systolic	Diastolic
Normal	120	80
Mild Hypertension	140-160	90-100
Moderate Hypertension	160-200	100-120
Severe Hypertension	Above 200	160-200

BLOOD PRESSURE LOG

NAME. _____

Date	AM		PM		Notes
	Blood pressure	Pulse	Blood pressure	Pulse	

Level of Severity	Systolic	Diastolic
Normal	120	80
Mild Hypertension	140-160	90-100
Moderate Hypertension	160-200	100-120
Severe Hypertension	Above 200	160-200

BLOOD PRESSURE LOG

NAME. ....

Date	AM		PM		Notes
	Blood pressure	Pulse	Blood pressure	Pulse	

Level of Severity	Systolic	Diastolic
Normal	120	80
Mild Hypertension	140-160	90-100
Moderate Hypertension	160-200	100-120
Severe Hypertension	Above 200	160-200

BLOOD PRESSURE LOG

NAME. _____

Date	AM		PM		Notes
	Blood pressure	Pulse	Blood pressure	Pulse	

Level of Severity	Systolic	Diastolic
Normal	120	80
Mild Hypertension	140-160	90-100
Moderate Hypertension	160-200	100-120
Severe Hypertension	Above 200	160-200

BLOOD PRESSURE LOG

NAME. _____

Date	AM		PM		Notes
	Blood pressure	Pulse	Blood pressure	Pulse	

Level of Severity	Systolic	Diastolic
Normal	120	80
Mild Hypertension	140-160	90-100
Moderate Hypertension	160-200	100-120
Severe Hypertension	Above 200	160-200

BLOOD PRESSURE LOG

NAME.

Date	AM		PM		Notes
	Blood pressure	Pulse	Blood pressure	Pulse	

Level of Severity	Systolic	Diastolic
Normal	120	80
Mild Hypertension	140-160	90-100
Moderate Hypertension	160-200	100-120
Severe Hypertension	Above 200	160-200

BLOOD PRESSURE LOG

NAME.

Date	AM		PM		Notes
	Blood pressure	Pulse	Blood pressure	Pulse	

Level of Severity	Systolic	Diastolic
Normal	120	80
Mild Hypertension	140-160	90-100
Moderate Hypertension	160-200	100-120
Severe Hypertension	Above 200	160-200

BLOOD PRESSURE LOG

NAME. _____

Date	AM		PM		Notes
	Blood pressure	Pulse	Blood pressure	Pulse	

Level of Severity	Systolic	Diastolic
Normal	120	80
Mild Hypertension	140-160	90-100
Moderate Hypertension	160-200	100-120
Severe Hypertension	Above 200	160-200

Made in the USA
Monee, IL
12 January 2022